LIFE
Lessons

WITH MAX LUCADO

BOOKS OF
1 & 2 TIMOTHY
AND TITUS

AGELESS WISDOM FOR
YOUNG LEADERS

MAX LUCADO

Prepared by

THE LIVINGSTONE CORPORATION

THOMAS NELSON
Since 1798

NASHVILLE   DALLAS   MEXICO CITY   RIO DE JANEIRO   BEIJING

Life Lessons with Max Lucado—Books of 1 & 2 Timothy and Titus

Produced with the assistance of the Livingstone Corporation (www.livingstonecorp.com). Project staff includes Jake Barton, Joel Bartlett, Andy Culbertson, Mary Horner Collins, and Will Reaves.
Editor: Neil Wilson

Cover Art and Interior Design by Kirk Luttrell of the Livingstone Corporation
Interior Composition by Rachel Hawkins of the Livingstone Corporation

ISBN-10: 978-1-4185-0954-X

ISBN-13: 978-1-4185-0954-5

Printed in the United States of America.
09 10 11 QW 9 8 7 6 5 4

LIFE Lessons

WITH MAX LUCADO

CONTENTS

HOW TO
STUDY THE BIBLE

This is a peculiar book you are holding. Words crafted in another language. Deeds done in a distant era. Events recorded in a far-off land. Counsel offered to a foreign people. This is a peculiar book.

It's surprising that anyone reads it. It's too old. Some of its writings date back five thousand years. It's too bizarre. The book speaks of incredible floods, fires, earthquakes, and people with supernatural abilities. It's too radical. The Bible calls for undying devotion to a carpenter who called himself God's Son.

Logic says this book shouldn't survive. Too old, too bizarre, too radical.

The Bible has been banned, burned, scoffed, and ridiculed. Scholars have mocked it as foolish. Kings have branded it as illegal. A thousand times over, the grave has been dug and the dirge has begun, but somehow the Bible never stays in the grave. Not only has it survived; it has thrived. It is the single most popular book in all of history. It has been the best-selling book in the world for years!

There is no way on earth to explain it. Which perhaps is the only explanation. The answer? The Bible's durability is not found on earth; it is found in heaven. For the millions who have tested its claims and claimed its promises, there is but one answer: the Bible is God's book and God's voice.

As you read it, you would be wise to give some thought to two questions. What is the purpose of the Bible? and How do I study the Bible? Time spent reflecting on these two issues will greatly enhance your Bible study.

What is the purpose of the Bible?

Let the Bible itself answer that question.

Since you were a child you have known the Holy Scriptures which are able to make you wise. And that wisdom leads to salvation through faith in Christ Jesus. (2 Tim. 3:15 NCV)

The purpose of the Bible? Salvation. God's highest passion is to get his children home. His book, the Bible, describes his plan of salvation. The purpose of the Bible is to proclaim God's plan and passion to save his children.

That is the reason this book has endured through the centuries. It dares to tackle the toughest questions about life: Where do I go after I die? Is there a God? What do I do with my fears? The Bible offers answers to these crucial questions. It is the treasure map that leads us to God's highest treasure, eternal life.

But how do we use the Bible? Countless copies of Scripture sit unread on bookshelves and nightstands simply because people don't know how to read it. What can we do to make the Bible real in our lives?

The clearest answer is found in the words of Jesus. He promised:

Ask, and God will give to you. Search, and you will find. Knock, and the door will open for you. (Matt. 7:7 NCV)

The first step in understanding the Bible is asking God to help us. We should read prayerfully. If anyone understands God's Word, it is because of God and not the reader.

But the Helper will teach you everything and will cause you to remember all that I told you. The Helper is the Holy Spirit whom the Father will send in my name. (John 14:26 NCV)

Before reading the Bible, pray. Invite God to speak to you. Don't go to Scripture looking for your idea; go searching for his.

Not only should we read the Bible prayerfully; we should read it carefully. *Search and you will find* is the pledge. The Bible is not a newspaper to be skimmed but rather a mine to be quarried.

Search for it like silver, and hunt for it like hidden treasure. Then you will understand respect for the LORD, and you will find that you know God. (Prov. 2:4–5 NCV)

Any worthy find requires effort. The Bible is no exception. To understand the Bible you don't have to be brilliant, but you must be willing to roll up your sleeves and search.

Be a worker who is not ashamed and who uses the true teaching in the right way. (2 Tim. 2:15 NCV)

Here's a practical point. Study the Bible a bit at a time. Hunger is not satisfied by eating twenty-one meals in one sitting once a week. The body needs a steady diet to remain strong. So does the soul. When God sent food to his people in the wilderness, he didn't provide loaves already made. Instead, he sent them manna in the shape of *"thin flakes like frost . . . on the desert ground"* (Ex. 16:14 NCV).

God gave manna in limited portions. God sends spiritual food the same way. He opens the heavens with just enough nutrients for today's hunger. He provides "a command here, a command there. A rule here, a rule there. A little lesson here, a little lesson there" (Isa. 28:10 NCV).

Don't be discouraged if your reading reaps a small harvest. Some days a lesser portion is all that is needed. What is important is to search every day for that day's message. A steady diet of God's Word over a lifetime builds a healthy soul and mind.

A little girl returned from her first day at school. Her mom asked, "Did you learn anything?"

"Apparently not enough," the girl responded, "I have to go back tomorrow and the next day and the next . . ."

Such is the case with learning. And such is the case with Bible study. Understanding comes little by little over a lifetime.

There is a third step in understanding the Bible. After the asking and seeking comes the knocking. After you ask and search, then knock.

Knock, and the door will open for you. (Matt. 7:7 NCV)

To knock is to stand at God's door. To make yourself available. To climb the steps, cross the porch, stand at the doorway, and volunteer. Knocking goes beyond the realm of thinking and into the realm of acting.

To knock is to ask, What can I do? How can I obey? Where can I go?

It's one thing to know what to do. It's another to do it. But for those who do it, those who choose to obey, a special reward awaits them.

The truly happy are those who carefully study God's perfect law that makes people free, and they continue to study it. They do not forget what they heard, but they obey what God's teaching says. Those who do this will be made happy. (James 1:25 NCV)

What a promise. Happiness comes to those who do what they read! It's the same with medicine. If you only read the label but ignore the pills, it won't help. It's the same with food. If you only read the recipe but never cook, you won't be fed. And it's the same with the Bible. If you only read the words but never obey, you'll never know the joy God has promised.

Ask. Search. Knock. Simple, isn't it? Why don't you give it a try? If you do, you'll see why you are holding the most remarkable book in history.

INTRODUCTION TO THE BOOK OF 1 TIMOTHY

Watch a small boy follow his dad through the snow. He stretches to step where his dad stepped. Not an easy task. His small legs extend as far as they can so his feet can fall in his father's prints.

The father, seeing what the son is doing, smiles and begins taking shorter steps, so the son can follow.

It's a picture of discipleship.

In our faith we follow in someone's steps. A parent, a teacher, a hero—none of us is the first to walk the trail. All of us have someone we follow. In our faith we leave footprints to guide others. A child, a friend, a recent convert. None should be left to walk the trail alone.

It's the principle of discipleship.

Timothy didn't walk the trail alone. He followed in the steps of Paul, his father in the faith. Paul knew he was following. He also knew the snow was getting deep. So he slowed his pace to help. He penned a letter to Timothy, giving him practical advice on how to lead a church.

As a young minister, Timothy was faced with all sorts of challenges. Step-by-step, Paul patiently instructed him, and in doing so, he instructs us.

A few questions to consider as you read. Who are you following? When you get where you are going, will it be where you intended? Also, what kind of trail are you leaving? If someone follows your steps, will he or she arrive at the right place?

The message of 1 Timothy urges you: Watch your step.

CHRIST'S POWER TO SAVE

MAX LUCADO

REFLECTION

Our lives should be different because of our relationship with Christ. Think of someone whose life has dramatically changed since he or she became a believer. What's different since he or she encountered Christ? What's the same? What evidence of Christ's power do you see in that person's life?

SITUATION

Timothy was Paul's representative for a while in Ephesus. Paul had founded the church and had spent years teaching that congregation. Later, while under imprisonment and restrictions in Rome, Paul heard that Ephesus was undergoing upheaval because of false teachers. He sent Timothy as a living reminder of the apostle's message in a church that was struggling with false teaching. This was a daunting task for a young pastor, and Paul wrote this letter to instruct and encourage Timothy.

OBSERVATION

Read 1 Timothy 1:12–20 from the NCV or the NKJV.

NCV

¹²*I thank Christ Jesus our Lord, who gave me strength, because he trusted me and gave me this work of serving him.* ¹³*In the past I spoke against Christ and persecuted him and did all kinds of things to hurt him. But God showed me mercy, because I did not know what I was doing. I did not believe.* ¹⁴*But the grace of our Lord was fully given to me, and with that grace came the faith and love that are in Christ Jesus.*

¹⁵*What I say is true, and you should fully accept it: Christ Jesus came into the world to save sinners, of whom I am the worst.* ¹⁶*But I was given mercy so that in me, the worst of all sinners, Christ Jesus could show that he has patience without limit. His patience with me made me an example for those who would believe in him and have life forever.* ¹⁷*To the King that rules forever, who will never die, who cannot be seen, the only God, be honor and glory forever and ever. Amen.*

¹⁸*Timothy, my child, I am giving you a command that agrees with the prophecies that were given about you in the past. I tell you this so you can follow them and fight the good fight.* ¹⁹*Continue to have faith and do what you know is right. Some people have rejected this, and their faith has been shipwrecked.* ²⁰*Hymenaeus and Alexander have done that, and I have given them to Satan so they will learn not to speak against God.*

NKJV

¹²*And I thank Christ Jesus our Lord who has enabled me, because He counted me faithful, putting me into the ministry,* ¹³*although I was formerly a blasphemer, a persecutor, and an insolent man; but I obtained mercy because I did it ignorantly in unbelief.* ¹⁴*And the grace of our Lord was exceedingly abundant, with faith and love which are in Christ Jesus.* ¹⁵*This is a faithful saying and worthy of all acceptance, that Christ Jesus came into the world to save sinners, of whom I am chief.* ¹⁶*However, for this reason I obtained mercy, that in me first Jesus Christ might show all longsuffering, as a pattern to those who are going to believe on Him for everlasting life.* ¹⁷*Now to the King eternal, immortal, invisible, to God who alone is wise, be honor and glory forever and ever. Amen.*

¹⁸*This charge I commit to you, son Timothy, according to the prophecies previously made concerning you, that by them you may wage the good warfare,* ¹⁹*having faith and a good conscience, which some having rejected, concerning the faith have suffered shipwreck,* ²⁰*of whom are Hymenaeus and Alexander, whom I delivered to Satan that they may learn not to blaspheme.*

EXPLORATION

1. How does Paul's life serve as an example to us? How does Timothy's?

2. Why do we need God's mercy? Note how Paul explained the mercy he received (v. 13).

3. In what ways does God's plan of salvation demonstrate his grace?

4. What results when people refuse to continue in faith?

5. How was Timothy to "fight the good fight" of faith?

INSPIRATION

Before he encountered Christ, Paul had been somewhat of a hero among the Pharisees . . .

Blue-blooded and wild-eyed, this young zealot was hell-bent on keeping the kingdom pure—and that meant keeping the Christians out. He marched through the countryside like a general demanding that backslidden Jews salute the flag of the motherland or kiss their family and hopes good-bye.

All this came to a halt, however, on the shoulder of a highway . . . That's when someone slammed on the stadium lights, and he heard the voice. When he found out whose voice it was, his jaw hit the ground, and his body followed. He braced himself for the worst. He knew it was all over . . . He prayed that death would be quick and painless.

But all he got was silence and the first of a lifetime of surprises.

He ended up bewildered and befuddled in a borrowed bedroom. God left him there a few days with scales on his eyes so thick that the only direction he could look was inside himself. And he didn't like what he saw.

He saw himself for who he really was—to use his own words, the worst of sinners . . . Alone in the room with his sins on his conscience and blood on his hands, he asked to be cleansed. The legalist Saul was buried, and the liberator Paul was born. He was never the same afterwards. And neither was the world . . .

The message is gripping: Show a man his failures without Jesus, and the result will be found in the roadside gutter. Give a man religion without reminding him of his filth, and the result will be arrogance in a three-piece suit. But get the two in the same heart—get sin to meet Savior and Savior to meet sin—and the result just might be another Pharisee-turned-preacher who sets the world on fire.
(From *The Applause of Heaven* by Max Lucado)

REACTION

6. Why do we sometimes think that God could never love or accept us?

7. Why is it important for us to recognize our own sinfulness?

8. What hope does this passage offer to us when we feel hopeless? (Some other examples you may want to look at are Psalms 103:8–18; 139:13–18; John 3:16–18; Romans 8:31–39; and Ephesians 3:16–19.)

9. What insight does this passage offer about the character of Christ?

10. List several ways Christ demonstrates his power through people.

11. Name one person you can tell about Christ's power to save. Think through your "spheres of influence." (For example, work, neighborhoods, clubs, family members, friends, and anywhere else you may regularly encounter people who don't know Christ.)

LIFE LESSONS

The power of Christ was evident in Paul's conversion and his life. Although Paul was confident in his role as a mentor and model for Timothy and others, that confidence never flowed from his past or his performance. He always pointed to what Christ had done and what Christ was doing in his life as reasons to "imitate" him. He was honest about his past shortcomings and failures. The way Paul talked about his past gives us a powerful example of the importance of honestly presenting ourselves—flaws and all—when we talk to others about Christ.

DEVOTION

Lord, you are merciful and forgiving. You sacrificed your life to free us from the bondage of sin. Only you have the power to change our sinful hearts and draw us close to you. Remind us of our need for your transforming power, and give us grateful hearts for what you have done for us.

For more Bible passages on Christ's saving power, see Luke 19:10; John 3:17; Acts 4:12; 5:31; Romans 5:8–9; 7:24–25; 1 Timothy 1:15; Hebrews 9:14; 1 Peter 1:18–19; 1 John 4:14; Revelation 1:5.

To complete the books of 1 & 2 Timothy and Titus during this twelve-part study, read 1 Timothy 1:1–20.

JOURNALING

How has knowing Christ transformed my life? What can I do to thank him?

LESSON TWO

PRAYER AND
WORSHIP

MAX
LUCADO

REFLECTION

Identify what you like most about the worship service at your church. Think about the parts of a service that draw you into God's presence. What parts of your worship service would you immediately notice if they were left out?

SITUATION

By the time Paul wrote this letter to Timothy, he had already experienced the full breadth of the Roman Empire's legal and prison system. The apostle was aware of the power of Rome, and he countered that power with respect and honor. He knew that God was in control of and works through systems he places in the world—like governments. Paul's call through Timothy for believers to pray for kings is serious business. So are relationships throughout the church.

OBSERVATION

Read 1 Timothy 2:1–15 from the NCV or the NKJV.

NCV

¹First, I tell you to pray for all people, asking God for what they need and being thankful to him. ²Pray for rulers and for all who have authority so that we can have quiet and peaceful lives full of worship and respect for God. ³This is good, and it pleases God our Savior, ⁴who wants all people to be saved and to know the truth. ⁵There is one God and one way human beings can reach God. That way is through Christ Jesus, who is himself human. ⁶He gave himself as a payment to free all people. He is proof that came at the right time. ⁷That is why I was chosen to tell the Good News and to be an apostle. (I am telling the truth; I am not lying.) I was chosen to teach those who are not Jews to believe and to know the truth.

⁸So, I want the men everywhere to pray, lifting up their hands in a holy manner, without anger and arguments.

⁹Also, women should wear proper clothes that show respect and self-control, not using braided hair or gold or pearls or expensive clothes. ¹⁰Instead, they should do good deeds, which is right for women who say they worship God.

¹¹Let a woman learn by listening quietly and being ready to cooperate in everything. ¹²But I do not allow a woman to teach or to have authority over a man, but to listen quietly, ¹³because Adam was formed first and then Eve. ¹⁴And Adam was not tricked, but the woman was tricked and became a sinner. ¹⁵But she will be saved through having children if they continue in faith, love, and holiness, with self-control.

NKJV

¹Therefore I exhort first of all that supplications, prayers, intercessions, and giving of thanks be made for all men, ²for kings and all who are in authority, that we may lead a quiet and peaceable life in all godliness and reverence. ³For this is good and acceptable in the sight of God our Savior, ⁴who desires all men to be saved and to come to the knowledge of the truth. ⁵For there is one God and one Mediator between God and men, the Man Christ Jesus, ⁶who gave Himself a ransom for all, to be testified in due time, ⁷for which I was appointed a preacher and an apostle—I am speaking the truth in Christ and not lying—a teacher of the Gentiles in faith and truth.

⁸I desire therefore that the men pray everywhere, lifting up holy hands, without wrath and doubting; ⁹in like manner also, that the women adorn themselves in modest apparel, with propriety and moderation, not with braided hair or gold or pearls or costly clothing, ¹⁰but, which is proper for women professing godliness, with good works. ¹¹Let a woman learn in silence with all submission. ¹²And I do not permit a woman to teach or to have authority over a man, but to be in silence. ¹³For Adam was formed first, then Eve. ¹⁴And Adam was not deceived, but the woman being deceived, fell into transgression. ¹⁵Nevertheless she will be saved in childbearing if they continue in faith, love, and holiness, with self-control.

EXPLORATION

1. What kind of behavior pleases God?

2. What elements should characterize the prayers of God's people?

3. List ways we can show our respect and love for God.

4. What inappropriate behavior should we avoid? What basic standards is Paul using to address interpersonal and leadership issues?

5. What is wrong with focusing on outward appearances in worship?

INSPIRATION

Success sabotages the memories of the successful. Kings of the mountain forget who carried them up the trail.

The flea did. An old fable tells of an elephant lumbering across a wooden bridge suspended over a ravine. As the big animal crossed over the worn-out structure, it creaked and groaned under the elephant's weight. When he reached the other side, a flea that had nestled itself in the elephant's ear proclaimed, "Boy, did we shake that bridge!"

What a flea-brained declaration! But don't we do the same? The man who begged for help in medical school ten years ago is too busy to worship today. Back when the family struggled to make ends meet, they leaned on God for daily bread. Now that there is an extra car in the garage and jingle in the pocket, they haven't spoken to him in a while. In the early days of the church, the founding members spent hours in prayer. Today the church is large, well attended, well funded. Who needs to pray?

Success begets amnesia. Doesn't have to, however. God offers spiritual ginseng to help your memory. His prescription is simply "Know the purpose of success." Why did God help you succeed? So you can make him known. (From *It's Not About Me* by Max Lucado)

REACTION

6. What do we gain from spending time in prayer and worship? (This question can be answered with personal experience, but you can also consult other passages such as Psalm 32:6–7; Psalm 100:2–5; Philippians 4:6–7; James 5:13–16.)

7. By what process does God reveal his plans to his people? How do people reveal God to the world?

8. In what ways can practicing spiritual disciplines combat selfishness? (Spiritual disciplines include reading, memorizing, and meditating on the Bible; prayer; solitude and silence; fasting; giving; service to others; and singing songs of praise.)

9. Think about a time when you found it difficult to pray or worship. Why?

10. What steps can you take to eliminate the things that interfere with your worship?

11. How can we fight the temptation to focus more on appearances than on God in worship?

LIFE LESSONS

Believers gather together for the wonderful and serious business of being in God's presence. When they become distracted by power struggles or personal agendas, Christ's agenda for the world fades into the background. We are to pray for the world and witness to people. The way we treat them and the way we treat one another will have a huge impact on our effectiveness in sharing the gospel with them. What God has given us is never just for our self-enjoyment. Every gift can be used to represent the One who gave it. The world is watching.

DEVOTION

Holy Father, you deserve much more than we ever can give, but we ask that you would accept our worship and hear our prayers. Align our plans with your purposes, Father, through faithful prayer and sincere worship. Expose our selfishness, so that we may repent, receive your forgiveness, and grow in our knowledge of you. Draw us to you and increase our faith.

For more Bible passages on prayer and worship, see 1 Chronicles 16:28–29; Psalms 6:9; 95:6; Matthew 21:22; John 4:24; Acts 2:41–47; Philippians 4:6; 1 Timothy 2:8.

To complete the books of 1 & 2 Timothy and Titus during this twelve-part study, read 1 Timothy 2:1–15.

JOURNALING

In light of this passage, what changes do I need to make in my prayer and worship habits?

L E S S O N   T H R E E

SERVANT
LEADERSHIP

MAX
LUCADO

REFLECTION

Think of a leader in your church whom you admire. Identify, if you can, some of the formative experiences, training, or background that person has had. What positive character traits does this leader display?

SITUATION

Since part of Timothy's task was to identify and appoint leaders among the believers in Ephesus, Paul provided some guidelines. These guidelines for elders (bishops) have stood the test of time. They are not culturally bound but have been the standards by which the church has chosen and tested leaders through the centuries since Paul's writing.

OBSERVATION

Read 1 Timothy 3:1–16 from the NCV or the NKJV.

NCV

¹What I say is true: Anyone wanting to become an elder desires a good work. ²An elder must not give people a reason to criticize him, and he must have only one wife. He must be self-controlled, wise, respected by others, ready to welcome guests, and able to teach. ³He must not drink too much wine or like to fight, but rather be gentle and peaceable, not loving money. ⁴He must be a good family leader, having children who cooperate with full respect. ⁵(If someone does not know how to lead the family, how can that person take care of God's church?) ⁶But an elder must not be a new believer, or he might be too proud of himself and be judged guilty just as the devil was. ⁷An elder must also have the respect of people who are not in the church so he will not be criticized by others and caught in the devil's trap.

⁸In the same way, deacons must be respected by others, not saying things they do not mean. They must not drink too much wine or try to get rich by cheating others. ⁹With a clear conscience they must follow the secret of the faith that God made known to us. ¹⁰Test them first. Then let them serve as deacons if you find nothing wrong in them. ¹¹In the same way, women must be respected by others. They must not speak evil of others. They must be self-controlled and trustworthy in everything. ¹²Deacons must have only one wife and be good leaders of their children and their own families. ¹³Those who serve well as deacons are making an honorable place for themselves, and they will be very bold in their faith in Christ Jesus.

[14]Although I hope I can come to you soon, I am writing these things to you now.
[15]Then, even if I am delayed, you will know how to live in the family of God. That family is the church of the living God, the support and foundation of the truth. [16]Without doubt, the secret of our life of worship is great:

> He was shown to us in a human body,
>
> proved right in spirit,
>
> and seen by angels.
>
> He was preached to those who are not Jews,
>
> believed in by the world,
>
> and taken up in glory.

NKJV

[1]This is a faithful saying: If a man desires the position of a bishop, he desires a good work. [2]A bishop then must be blameless, the husband of one wife, temperate, sober-minded, of good behavior, hospitable, able to teach; [3]not given to wine, not violent, not greedy for money, but gentle, not quarrelsome, not covetous; [4]one who rules his own house well, having his children in submission with all reverence [5](for if a man does not know how to rule his own house, how will he take care of the church of God?); [6]not a novice, lest being puffed up with pride he fall into the same condemnation as the devil. [7]Moreover he must have a good testimony among those who are outside, lest he fall into reproach and the snare of the devil.

[8]Likewise deacons must be reverent, not double-tongued, not given to much wine, not greedy for money, [9]holding the mystery of the faith with a pure conscience. [10]But let these also first be tested; then let them serve as deacons, being found blameless. [11]Likewise their wives must be reverent, not slanderers, temperate, faithful in all things. [12]Let deacons be the husbands of one wife, ruling their children and their own houses well. [13]For those who have served well as deacons obtain for themselves a good standing and great boldness in the faith which is in Christ Jesus.

[14]These things I write to you, though I hope to come to you shortly; [15]but if I am delayed, I write so that you may know how you ought to conduct yourself in the house of God, which is the church of the living God, the pillar and ground of the truth. [16]And without controversy great is the mystery of godliness:

> God was manifested in the flesh,
>
> Justified in the Spirit,
>
> Seen by angels,
>
> Preached among the Gentiles,
>
> Believed on in the world,
>
> Received up in glory.

EXPLORATION

1. List some qualifications that Paul outlined in this passage for church leaders.

2. What practices should elders and deacons avoid?

3. Why is it important for church leaders to manage their families well?

4. What is the danger in giving a new believer a position of leadership in the church?

5. Why is it necessary for churches to have high expectations and standards for their leaders?

INSPIRATION

The temperature is in the twenties. The chill factor is single digit. The West Texas wind stings the ears, and frozen grass cracks beneath the step. It is a cold December day. Even the cattle are smart enough to stay in the barn on mornings like this.

Then what am I doing outside? What am I doing standing in a ditch, ankle deep in water, hunkered over a leaking pipe? And, most of all, why aren't the three guys in the truck helping me? Why are they in there while I'm out here? Why are they warm while I'm cold? Why are they dry while I'm wet?

The answer is found in two words: *pecking order*.

We can thank Norwegian naturalists for the term. They are the ones who studied the barnyard caste system. By counting the number of times chicken give and receive pecks, we can discern a chain of command. The alpha bird does most of the pecking, and the omega bird gets pecked. The rest of the chickens are somewhere in between.

That day in the oil field, our alpha bird was the crew chief. Beneath him was a former foreman and beneath the foreman, an illegal immigrant. I was the omega bird. College students on Christmas break come in last . . .

I understood the pecking order. You do too. You know the system. Pecking orders are a part of life. And, to an extent, they should be. We need to know who is in charge. Ranking systems can clarify our roles. The problem with pecking orders is not the order. The problem is with the pecking.

For that reason God says that love has no place for pecking orders. Jesus won't tolerate such thinking. Such barnyard mentality may fly on the farm but not in his kingdom. Just listen to what he says about the alpha birds of his day (Matt. 23:5–7) . . . Jesus blasts the top birds of the church, those who roost at the top of the spiritual ladder and spread their plumes of robes, titles, jewelry, and choice seats. Jesus won't stand for it. It's easy to see why. How can I love others if my eyes are only on me? How can I point to God if I'm pointing at me? And, worse still, how can someone see God if I keep fanning my own tail feathers?

Jesus has no room for pecking orders. Love "does not boast, it is not proud" (1 Cor. 13:4 NIV).

His solution to man-made caste systems? A change of direction. In a world of upward mobility, choose downward servility. Go down, not up. "Regard one another as more important than yourselves" (Phil. 2:3 NASB). That's what Jesus did. He flip-flopped the pecking order. While others were going up, he was going down. (From *A Love Worth Giving* by Max Lucado)

REACTION

6. In practical terms, describe what you think it means to be a servant leader.

7. What steps can leaders take to guard against the sins of pride and arrogance?

8. In what way do you think your church could improve the way it chooses leaders?

9. Why do you think some people hesitate to accept leadership positions in the church?

10. How have you benefited from the ministry of your church leaders?

11. In what concrete way can you encourage a leader in your church this week?

LIFE LESSONS

Always find a place of service within the church. If you are a leader who must identify abilities and skills in others, do your homework. Observe them carefully—not critically. Your primary task is not to find faults but to develop a list of their best qualities. Before you ask someone to lead, be prepared to tell that individual several positive reasons why you have approached him or her. When you are approached by someone in the church and asked to fill a role or take on a duty, consider the opportunity seriously. Seek to discover what that person saw in you that made him or her think you were suited for the job. The answer may allow you to discover how others see your skills or character.

DEVOTION

Thank you, Father, for sending your Son to show us what it means to be a servant. Make us more like Jesus. Keep us from vying for position and power. Help us to grow in holiness and humility. And above all else, keep our eyes focused on you.

For more Bible passages on leadership, see Matthew 20:25–28; Luke 22:24–27; 1 Corinthians 3:1–9; 2 Timothy 2:24–25; 1 Peter 5:1–6.

To complete the books of 1 & 2 Timothy and Titus during this twelve-part study, read 1 Timothy 3:1–16.

JOURNALING

Which of the characteristics described in this passage do I need to cultivate in my own life? How?

BELIEVING
THE TRUTH

MAX
LUCADO

REFLECTION

Some people have been taught that it's wrong to have questions or doubts about their faith. But there's nothing wrong with questioning, as long as you look for answers in the right place. The Bible is the source of all truth and all wisdom and is a book that has withstood the scrutiny of generations. Think of a time when you had questions about your Christian faith. How did you deal with your doubts?

SITUATION

Once he had given Timothy guidelines for choosing leaders within the church, Paul moved on to challenge his disciple to live well in the sight of the watching church. He wanted Timothy to understand the actions and attitudes that mark a life that is committed to Christ.

OBSERVATION

Read 1 Timothy 4:1–16 from the NCV or the NKJV.

NCV

¹Now the Holy Spirit clearly says that in the later times some people will stop believing the faith. They will follow spirits that lie and teachings of demons. ²Such teachings come from the false words of liars whose consciences are destroyed as if by a hot iron. ³They forbid people to marry and tell them not to eat certain foods which God created to be eaten with thanks by people who believe and know the truth. ⁴Everything God made is good, and nothing should be refused if it is accepted with thanks, ⁵because it is made holy by what God has said and by prayer.

6By telling these things to the brothers and sisters, you will be a good servant of Christ Jesus. You will be made strong by the words of the faith and the good teaching which you have been following. 7But do not follow foolish stories that disagree with God's truth, but train yourself to serve God. 8Training your body helps you in some ways, but serving God helps you in every way by bringing you blessings in this life and in the future life, too. 9What I say is true, and you should fully accept it. 10This is why we work and struggle: We hope in the living God who is the Savior of all people, especially of those who believe.

11Command and teach these things. 12Do not let anyone treat you as if you are unimportant because you are young. Instead, be an example to the believers with your words, your actions, your love, your faith, and your pure life. 13Until I come, continue to read the Scriptures to the people, strengthen them, and teach them. 14Use the gift you have, which was given to you through prophecy when the group of elders laid their hands on you. 15Continue to do those things; give your life to doing them so your progress may be seen by everyone. 16Be careful in your life and in your teaching. If you continue to live and teach rightly, you will save both yourself and those who listen to you.

NKJV

1Now the Spirit expressly says that in latter times some will depart from the faith, giving heed to deceiving spirits and doctrines of demons, 2speaking lies in hypocrisy, having their own conscience seared with a hot iron, 3forbidding to marry, and commanding to abstain from foods which God created to be received with thanksgiving by those who believe and know the truth. 4For every creature of God is good, and nothing is to be refused if it is received with thanksgiving; 5for it is sanctified by the word of God and prayer.

6If you instruct the brethren in these things, you will be a good minister of Jesus Christ, nourished in the words of faith and of the good doctrine which you have carefully followed. 7But reject profane and old wives' fables, and exercise yourself toward godliness. 8For bodily exercise profits a little, but godliness is profitable for all things, having promise of the life that now is and of that which is to come. 9This is a faithful saying and worthy of all acceptance. 10For to this end we both labor and suffer reproach, because we trust in the living God, who is the Savior of all men, especially of those who believe. 11These things command and teach.

12Let no one despise your youth, but be an example to the believers in word, in conduct, in love, in spirit, in faith, in purity. 13Till I come, give attention to reading, to exhortation, to doctrine. 14Do not neglect the gift that is in you, which was given to you by prophecy with the laying on of the hands of the eldership. 15Meditate on these things; give yourself entirely to them, that your progress may be evident to all. 16Take heed to yourself and to the doctrine. Continue in them, for in doing this you will save both yourself and those who hear you.

EXPLORATION

1. What keeps people from believing the truth of the gospel?

2. What threat do false teachers pose to the church? How do true teachers build up the church?

3. What happens when distortions of the truth go unchecked?

4. What can believers do to protect themselves from false teaching?

5. In what ways can careful living and right teaching save people?

INSPIRATION

Jesus' heart was pure. The Savior was adored by thousands, yet content to live a simple life. He was cared for by women (Luke 8:1–3), yet never accused of lustful thoughts; scorned by his own creation, but willing to forgive them before they even requested his mercy. Peter, who traveled with Jesus for three and a half years, described him as a "lamb unblemished and spotless" (1 Pet. 1:19 NASB). After spending the same amount of time with Jesus, John concluded, "And in him is no sin" (John 3:5 NIV).

Jesus' heart was peaceful. The disciples fretted over the need to feed the thousands, but not Jesus. He thanked God for the problem. The disciples shouted for fear in the storm, but not Jesus. He slept through it. Peter drew his sword to fight the soldiers, but not Jesus. He lifted his hand to heal. His heart was at peace. When his disciples abandoned him, did he pout and go home? When Peter denied him, did Jesus lose his temper? When the soldiers spit in his face, did he breathe fire in theirs? Far from it. He was at peace. He forgave them. He refused to be guided by vengeance.

He refused to be guided by anything other than his high call. Jesus' heart was purposeful. Most lives aim at nothing in particular and achieve it. Jesus aimed at one goal—to save humanity from its sin. He could summarize his life with one sentence: "The Son of man came to seek out and to save the lost" (Luke 19:10 NRSV). Jesus was so focused on his task that he knew when to say, "My time has not yet come" (John 2:4 NCV) and when to say, "It is finished" (John 19:30 NCV). But he was not so focused on his goal that he was unpleasant.

Quite the contrary. How pleasant were his thoughts! Children couldn't resist Jesus. He could find beauty in lilies, joy in worship, and possibilities in problems. He would spend days with multitudes of sick people and still feel sorry for them. He spent over three decades wading through the muck and mire of our sin yet still saw enough beauty in us to die for our mistakes. (From *Just Like Jesus Devotional* by Max Lucado)

REACTION

6. How did Jesus' life, as an example of righteous living, draw people to him

7. Why are we prone to unbelief? How do the details of our lives reflect the things we truly believe?

8. What kind of questioning can strengthen a person's faith?

9. List several practices or activities that promote spiritual growth.

10. When can you devote more time to doing the things that strengthen your Christian beliefs? (Note: Sometimes we feel we don't have more time to do anything. It can be helpful to do a "time inventory." For one week, write down how you spend your time each day. At the end of the week, look back at how you spent your time. You may be surprised at how much time you spend doing things like watching television, reading the newspaper, or other leisure activities.)

11. How can you help someone who you know is questioning his or her beliefs?

LIFE LESSONS

Timothy was a young man expected to lead. He had to step up spiritually. But he also had personal struggles, doubts, and challenges to overcome. In other words, Timothy was an awful lot like us. The way Paul wrote to him (and us) makes it clear that our lives in Christ will stretch us constantly. We will be required to live beyond our human abilities. The degree to which we grow will be related to the degree to which we allow Christ to grow in us. Like Timothy, we need to learn and practice the central discipline of godliness, even as we are pursuing other good practices in life.

DEVOTION

Father, forgive us for doubting you. You have proven your existence and your love for us time and time again. Give us the desire to keep working and struggling to know you better. We ask you, Father, to confirm our beliefs and strengthen our faith in you.

For more Bible passages on believing the truth, see Mark 1:15; John 14:10–12; 20:31; Galatians 3:2; 1 Thessalonians 4:14; Hebrews 11:6; 1 John 4:1–6.

To complete the books of 1 & 2 Timothy and Titus during this twelve-part study, read 1 Timothy 4:1–16.

JOURNALING

What questions do I have about the Bible, Jesus, or God?

LESSON FIVE

RELATIONSHIPS

MAX
LUCADO

REFLECTION

Relationships come in all shapes and sizes. We all have people in our lives who are easy to love, and others whom we simply tolerate. What is the best advice you have heard on resolving conflicts in relationships?

SITUATION

After encouraging Timothy in chapter 4 to be careful in his life and in his teaching, Paul continued his personal counsel to Timothy about relating to the members of his church. In particular, these guidelines define for Timothy how he should treat the older, younger, and needy folks under his care.

OBSERVATION

Read 1 Timothy 5:1–21 from the NCV or the NKJV.

NCV

¹*Do not speak angrily to an older man, but plead with him as if he were your father. Treat younger men like brothers, ²older women like mothers, and younger women like sisters. Always treat them in a pure way.*

³*Take care of widows who are truly widows. ⁴But if a widow has children or grand-children, let them first learn to do their duty to their own family and to repay their parents or grandparents. That pleases God. ⁵The true widow, who is all alone, puts her hope in God and continues to pray night and day for God's help. ⁶But the widow who uses her life to please herself is really dead while she is alive. ⁷Tell the believers to do these things so that no one can criticize them. ⁸Whoever does not care for his own relatives, especially his own family members, has turned against the faith and is worse than someone who does not believe in God.*

⁹*To be on the list of widows, a woman must be at least sixty years old. She must have been faithful to her husband. ¹⁰She must be known for her good works—works such as raising her children, welcoming strangers, washing the feet of God's people, helping those in trouble, and giving her life to do all kinds of good deeds.*

¹¹*But do not put younger widows on that list. After they give themselves to Christ, they are pulled away from him by their physical needs, and then they want to marry again.*

[12]They will be judged for not doing what they first promised to do. [13]Besides that, they learn to waste their time, going from house to house. And they not only waste their time but also begin to gossip and busy themselves with other people's lives, saying things they should not say. [14]So I want the younger widows to marry, have children, and manage their homes. Then no enemy will have any reason to criticize them. [15]But some have already turned away to follow Satan.

[16]If any woman who is a believer has widows in her family, she should care for them herself. The church should not have to care for them. Then it will be able to take care of those who are truly widows.

[17]The elders who lead the church well should receive double honor, especially those who work hard by speaking and teaching, [18]because the Scripture says: "When an ox is working in the grain, do not cover its mouth to keep it from eating," and "A worker should be given his pay."

[19]Do not listen to someone who accuses an elder, without two or three witnesses. [20]Tell those who continue sinning that they are wrong. Do this in front of the whole church so that the others will have a warning.

[21]Before God and Christ Jesus and the chosen angels, I command you to do these things without showing favor of any kind to anyone.

NKJV

[1]Do not rebuke an older man, but exhort him as a father, younger men as brothers, [2]older women as mothers, younger as sisters, with all purity.

[3]Honor widows who are really widows. [4]But if any widow has children or grandchildren, let them first learn to show piety at home and to repay their parents; for this is good and acceptable before God. [5]Now she who is really a widow, and left alone, trusts in God and continues in supplications and prayers night and day. [6]But she who lives in pleasure is dead while she lives. [7]And these things command, that they may be blameless. [8]But if anyone does not provide for his own, and especially for those of his household, he has denied the faith and is worse than an unbeliever.

[9]Do not let a widow under sixty years old be taken into the number, and not unless she has been the wife of one man, [10]well reported for good works: if she has brought up children, if she has lodged strangers, if she has washed the saints' feet, if she has relieved the afflicted, if she has diligently followed every good work.

[11]But refuse the younger widows; for when they have begun to grow wanton against Christ, they desire to marry, [12]having condemnation because they have cast off their first faith. [13]And besides they learn to be idle, wandering about from house to house, and not only idle but also gossips and busybodies, saying things which they ought not. [14]Therefore I desire that the younger widows marry, bear children, manage the house, give no opportunity to the adversary to speak reproachfully. [15]For some have already turned aside after Satan. [16]If any believing man or woman has widows, let them relieve them, and do not let the church be burdened, that it may relieve those who are really widows.

¹⁷*Let the elders who rule well be counted worthy of double honor, especially those who labor in the word and doctrine.* ¹⁸*For the Scripture says, "You shall not muzzle an ox while it treads out the grain," and, "The laborer is worthy of his wages."* ¹⁹*Do not receive an accusation against an elder except from two or three witnesses.* ²⁰*Those who are sinning rebuke in the presence of all, that the rest also may fear.*

²¹*I charge you before God and the Lord Jesus Christ and the elect angels that you observe these things without prejudice, doing nothing with partiality.*

EXPLORATION

1. How should believers treat one another? (The Bible is filled with passages that tell us how we should treat one another. For more examples, look at John 15:12–13; Romans 12:9–21; Romans 15:1–2; Galatians 6:9–10; Ephesians 4:25–5:2; Philippians 2:3–4; Colossians 3:12–17; and 1 John 3:16–18.) How does this passage confirm and expand those others?

2. What guidelines should believers follow in caring for needy people?

3. What responsibilities should the church not accept?

4. Explain what it means to care properly for one's family.

INSPIRATION

"Give me a word picture to describe a relative in your life who really bugs you."

I was asking the question of a half-dozen friends sitting around a lunch table. They all gave me one of those what-in-the-world? expressions. So I explained.

"I keep meeting people who can't deal with somebody in their family. Either their mother-in-law is a witch or their uncle is a bum or they have a father who treats them like they were never born." . . .

"Tar baby in Brer Rabbit," someone responded. Everyone understood the reference except me. I didn't remember the story of Brer Rabbit. I asked for the short version. Wily Fox played a trick on Brer Rabbit. The fox made a doll out of tar and stuck it on the side of the road. When Rabbit saw the tar baby, he thought it was a person and stopped to visit.

It was a one-sided conversation. The tar baby's silence bothered the rabbit. He couldn't stand to be next to someone and not communicate with him. So in his frustration he hit the tar baby and stuck to it. He hit the tar baby again with the other hand and, you guessed it, the other hand got stuck.

"That's how we are with difficult relatives," my fable-using friend explained. "We're stuck to someone we can't communicate with." . . .

You've probably got a tar baby in your life, someone you can't talk to and can't walk away from. A mother who whines, an uncle who slurps his soup, or a sister who flaunts her figure. A dad who is still waiting for you to get a real job or a mother-in-law who wonders why her daughter married you.

Tar-baby relationships—stuck together but falling apart . . .

Why does life get so relatively difficult? If we expect anyone to be sensitive to our needs, it is our family members. When we hurt physically, we want our family to respond. When we struggle emotionally, we want our family to know.

But sometimes they act like they don't know. Sometimes they act like they don't care.

I can't assure you that your family will ever give you the blessing you seek, but I know God will. Let God give you what your family doesn't. If your earthly father doesn't affirm you, then let your heavenly Father take his place.

How do you do that? By emotionally accepting God as your father. You see, it's one thing to accept him as Lord, another to recognize him as Savior—but it's another matter entirely to accept him as Father.

To recognize God as Lord is to acknowledge that he is sovereign and supreme in the universe. To accept him as Savior is to accept his gift of salvation offered on the cross. To regard him as Father is to go a step further. Ideally, a father is the one in your life who provides and protects. That is exactly what God has done . . .

God has proven himself as a faithful father. Now it falls to us to be trusting children. Let God give you what your family doesn't. Let him fill the void others have left. (From *He Still Moves Stones* by Max Lucado)

REACTION

5. Why do we find it difficult to get along with the people we love?

6. What are some justifications you've heard for shirking family responsibilities?

7. In what way does caring for one's family demonstrate a person's commitment and love for Christ?

8. How has your relationship with God affected your relationships with others? Consider the issue of dependence. The Bible makes it clear that as Christians we are part of the body of Christ, and we are meant to live our lives in an interdependence on other believers.

9. Name one principle from this passage that could help you relate better with others.

10. How can you apply this principle to one relationship this week?

LIFE LESSONS

As we and other people pass through stages of life, our relationships change. These role-based relationships make up a great deal of life. One of the key words we need to define and practice in each kind of relationship is the word *honor*. We don't owe the same honor to all, but to each person we can offer some kind of honor. Who and how will you honor the people in your life today?

DEVOTION

Father, sometimes the difficulties and demands of relationships can be overwhelming. Help us fulfill our responsibilities to the people you have placed in our lives. Give us the wisdom to deal with conflict and the strength to cope with disappointment. May we treat others with love and respect by following the practical guidelines in your Word.

For more Bible passages on relationships, see Psalm 133:1–3; Proverbs 18:24; 21:9, 19; Ephesians 2:14–22; 1 Thessalonians 5:12–13; Hebrews 12:14; 13:1–4; 1 Peter 3:1–8; 1 John 2:9–11; 3:11–18; 4:20–21.

To complete the books of 1 & 2 Timothy and Titus during this twelve-part study, read 1 Timothy 5:1–25.

LIFE LESSONS WITH MAX LUCADO

JOURNALING

What do others learn about Jesus from the way I treat my friends and relatives?

LESSON SIX

CONTENTMENT

MAX
LUCADO

REFLECTION

What brings you the most happiness in life? Don't just give the expected Sunday school answer. This is personal. Avoid describing what you think should bring you happiness or what you would like to bring you happiness. Be open and honest in your answer.

SITUATION

As Paul neared the end of this letter, he drew Timothy's attention again to the importance of a life of godliness and contentment. Paul told Timothy that he had expectations for his young protégé, and he was eager to see Timothy live out his potential as a man of God.

OBSERVATION

Read 1 Timothy 6:6–19 from the NCV or the NKJV.

NCV

6Serving God does make us very rich, if we are satisfied with what we have. 7We brought nothing into the world, so we can take nothing out. 8But, if we have food and clothes, we will be satisfied with that. 9Those who want to become rich bring temptation to themselves and are caught in a trap. They want many foolish and harmful things that ruin and destroy people. 10The love of money causes all kinds of evil. Some people have left the faith, because they wanted to get more money, but they have caused themselves much sorrow.

¹¹*But you, man of God, run away from all those things. Instead, live in the right way, serve God, have faith, love, patience, and gentleness. ¹²Fight the good fight of faith, grabbing hold of the life that continues forever. You were called to have that life when you confessed the good confession before many witnesses. ¹³In the sight of God, who gives life to everything, and of Christ Jesus, I give you a command. Christ Jesus made the good confession when he stood before Pontius Pilate. ¹⁴Do what you were commanded to do without wrong or blame until our Lord Jesus Christ comes again. ¹⁵God will make that happen at the right time. He is the blessed and only Ruler, the King of all kings and the Lord of all lords. ¹⁶He is the only One who never dies. He lives in light so bright no one can go near it. No one has ever seen God, or can see him. May honor and power belong to God forever. Amen.*

¹⁷*Command those who are rich with things of this world not to be proud. Tell them to hope in God, not in their uncertain riches. God richly gives us everything to enjoy. ¹⁸Tell the rich people to do good, to be rich in doing good deeds, to be generous and ready to share. ¹⁹By doing that, they will be saving a treasure for themselves as a strong foundation for the future. Then they will be able to have the life that is true life.*

NKJV

⁶*Now godliness with contentment is great gain. ⁷For we brought nothing into this world, and it is certain we can carry nothing out. ⁸And having food and clothing, with these we shall be content. ⁹But those who desire to be rich fall into temptation and a snare, and into many foolish and harmful lusts which drown men in destruction and perdition. ¹⁰For the love of money is a root of all kinds of evil, for which some have strayed from the faith in their greediness, and pierced themselves through with many sorrows.*

¹¹*But you, O man of God, flee these things and pursue righteousness, godliness, faith, love, patience, gentleness. ¹²Fight the good fight of faith, lay hold on eternal life, to which you were also called and have confessed the good confession in the presence of many witnesses. ¹³I urge you in the sight of God who gives life to all things, and before Christ Jesus who witnessed the good confession before Pontius Pilate, ¹⁴that you keep this commandment without spot, blameless until our Lord Jesus Christ's appearing, ¹⁵which He will manifest in His own time, He who is the blessed and only Potentate, the King of kings and Lord of lords, ¹⁶who alone has immortality, dwelling in unapproachable light, whom no man has seen or can see, to whom be honor and everlasting power. Amen.*

¹⁷*Command those who are rich in this present age not to be haughty, nor to trust in uncertain riches but in the living God, who gives us richly all things to enjoy. ¹⁸Let them do good, that they be rich in good works, ready to give, willing to share, ¹⁹storing up for themselves a good foundation for the time to come, that they may lay hold on eternal life.*

EXPLORATION

I. In what way does serving God make a person "rich"?

2. Why is it important to realize that our earthly goods will be worthless in eternity?

3. What are some of the dangers associated with seeking material wealth?

4. Define contentment, particularly as this passage refers to it. Explain how a person can find true contentment.

5. What warnings does Scripture give to rich people? (See, for example, Proverbs 28:20; Ecclesiastes 5:12; Matthew 19:16–26; Luke 6:24; 12:13–21; and James 5:1–6.)

INSPIRATION

Satisfied? That is one thing we are not. We are not satisfied.

We push back from the Thanksgiving table and pat our round bellies. "I'm satisfied," we declare. But look at us a few hours later, back in the kitchen picking the meat from the bone.

We wake up after a good night's rest and hop out of bed. We couldn't go back to sleep if someone paid us. We are satisfied—for a while. But look at us a dozen or so hours later, crawling back in the sheets.

We take a vacation of a lifetime. For years we planned. For years we saved. And off we go. We satiate ourselves with sun, fun, and good food. But we are not even on the way home before we dread the end of the trip and begin planning another.

We are not satisfied.

As a child we say, "If only I were a teenager." As a teen we say, "If only I were an adult." As an adult, "If only I were married." As a spouse, "If only I had kids." As a parent, "If only my kids were grown." In an empty house, "If only the kids would visit." As a retiree in the rocking chair with stiff joints and fading sight, "If only I were a child again."

We are not satisfied. Contentment is a difficult virtue. Why?

Because there is nothing on earth that can satisfy our deepest longing. We long to see God. The leaves of life are rustling with the rumor that we will—and we won't be satisfied until we do. (From *When God Whispers Your Name* by Max Lucado)

REACTION

6. Why is it difficult to be satisfied with what we have? What are some of the warning signs of discontent?

7. In what way can a desire for more money destroy a person?

8. List the benefits of sharing your wealth with others. Also list some specific ways that you can share your wealth with others.

9. Why do you think people believe that money brings security and fulfillment?

10. Why is it tempting to trust in our wealth instead of God?

11. On a scale of 1 to 10 (10 being very content), how content are you with what you have?

LIFE LESSONS

If godliness describes how much we are like Christ, reflecting his actions and character, then contentment describes the ways we reflect his attitude. We don't take our cues for peace and satisfaction primarily from our environment, but from Jesus. We aren't trying to copy Jesus mechanically, but are asking him to work out his character within us. The kind of contentment Paul is urging Timothy (and us) to have is the kind of contentment that develops as a by-product of knowing Jesus Christ intimately. How will you participate in your relationship with Christ today?

DEVOTION

Heavenly Father, when we are dissatisfied with what we have, open our eyes to the riches we have in you. Loosen our grip on our wealth by showing us ways to invest in eternal treasures. Teach us to share what we have and to enjoy the simple pleasures of life.

For more Bible passages on contentment, see Psalm 63:5; Proverbs 19:23; Ecclesiastes 5:10–12; Luke 6:20–23; Philippians 4:10–13; Hebrews 13:5.

To complete the books of 1 & 2 Timothy and Titus during this twelve-part study, read 1 Timothy 6:1–21.

JOURNALING

In what area of my life do I need God's help to be more content?

Jeremiah & Joshua — Bagdad
Hazel Feeling Bad
Don Holland
Duane & Carol Barschdorf
Pat Burkhalter
Bruce Brockman (Cheryl — ms)
Dave Bossertt

INTRODUCTION TO THE BOOK OF 2 TIMOTHY

"I have kept the faith."

They have taken everything else. They have taken Paul's freedom—he's locked in a Roman prison. They have taken his possessions—he hasn't even a shawl to keep him warm. They have taken his churches—he will not see them again. They have taken his future—he is sentenced to die.

What do you have left, Paul? What do you have left to show for your life? Had you stayed a Jew in Jerusalem, you'd have a seat of status and a house of retirement. Had you been more compromising, you might have gone unnoticed by the Romans. Had you been less passionate, you might have pastored a church and stayed in one city. But you were too convinced to compromise—too convicted to stay home.

And now, with the verdict rendered and the end in sight, what do you have left?

The old apostle leans forward with eyes twinkling and says, "I have kept the faith."

That was the heart of the apostle. And that is the heart of this epistle. As far as we know, this is the last one he ever wrote. Paul picks up his pen one final time. He knows the end is near, "I am being poured out like a drink offering," he tells Timothy, his son in the faith. But he has no regrets, only counsel—practical, inspirational counsel for young Timothy, who has been left to lead the church in Ephesus. His tenderness for the young minister peeks out from behind every word. "Make every effort," he urges, "to give yourself to God as the kind of person he will accept. Be a worker who is not ashamed and who uses the true teaching in the right way" (2:15 NCV).

Timothy never had another teacher like Paul. The world has never had another teacher like Paul. He was convinced of two facts—he was once lost but then saved. He spent a lifetime telling every person who would listen.

In the end, it cost him everything. For in the end, all he had was his faith. But in the end, his faith was all he needed.

STRENGTH
IN
SUFFERING

MAX
LUCADO

REFLECTION

Are there people who have been sources of encouragement to you during a difficult time in your life? Remember what they did, what they said, and the way they timed their involvement with you. How did they encourage you?

SITUATION

Almost alone in prison, facing the end of life, Paul wrote his last letter to Timothy. Their years as a team had been rich, and this adds depth and emotion to his comments. Some of the language Paul uses is the language of old friends. Paul had some precious final words to pass on to Timothy, and to us He began by reviewing his present situation and encouraging Timothy.

OBSERVATION

Read 2 Timothy 1:1–18 from the NCV or the NKJV.

NCV

¹From Paul, an apostle of Christ Jesus by the will of God. God sent me to tell about the promise of life that is in Christ Jesus.

²To Timothy, a dear child to me:

Grace, mercy, and peace to you from God the Father and Christ Jesus our Lord.

³I thank God as I always mention you in my prayers, day and night. I serve him, doing what I know is right as my ancestors did. ⁴Remembering that you cried for me, I want very much to see you so I can be filled with joy. ⁵I remember your true faith. That faith first lived in your grandmother Lois and in your mother Eunice, and I know you now have that same faith. ⁶This is why I remind you to keep using the gift God gave you when I laid my hands on you. Now let it grow, as a small flame grows into a fire. ⁷God did not give us a spirit that makes us afraid but a spirit of power and love and self-control.

[8]*So do not be ashamed to tell people about our Lord Jesus, and do not be ashamed of me, in prison for the Lord. But suffer with me for the Good News. God, who gives us the strength to do that,* [9]*saved us and made us his holy people. That was not because of anything we did ourselves but because of God's purpose and grace. That grace was given to us through Christ Jesus before time began,* [10]*but it is now shown to us by the coming of our Savior Christ Jesus. He destroyed death, and through the Good News he showed us the way to have life that cannot be destroyed.* [11]*I was chosen to tell that Good News and to be an apostle and a teacher.* [12]*I am suffering now because I tell the Good News, but I am not ashamed, because I know Jesus, the One in whom I have believed. And I am sure he is able to protect what he has trusted me with until that day.* [13]*Follow the pattern of true teachings that you heard from me in faith and love, which are in Christ Jesus.* [14]*Protect the truth that you were given; protect it with the help of the Holy Spirit who lives in us.*

[15]*You know that everyone in the country of Asia has left me, even Phygelus and Hermogenes.* [16]*May the Lord show mercy to the family of Onesiphorus, who has often helped me and was not ashamed that I was in prison.* [17]*When he came to Rome, he looked eagerly for me until he found me.* [18]*May the Lord allow him to find mercy from the Lord on that day. You know how many ways he helped me in Ephesus.*

NKJV

[1]*Paul, an apostle of Jesus Christ by the will of God, according to the promise of life which is in Christ Jesus,*

[2]*To Timothy, a beloved son:*

Grace, mercy, and peace from God the Father and Christ Jesus our Lord.

[3]*I thank God, whom I serve with a pure conscience, as my forefathers did, as without ceasing I remember you in my prayers night and day,* [4]*greatly desiring to see you, being mindful of your tears, that I may be filled with joy,* [5]*when I call to remembrance the genuine faith that is in you, which dwelt first in your grandmother Lois and your mother Eunice, and I am persuaded is in you also.* [6]*Therefore I remind you to stir up the gift of God which is in you through the laying on of my hands.* [7]*For God has not given us a spirit of fear, but of power and of love and of a sound mind.*

[8]*Therefore do not be ashamed of the testimony of our Lord, nor of me His prisoner, but share with me in the sufferings for the gospel according to the power of God,* [9]*who has saved us and called us with a holy calling, not according to our works, but according to His own purpose and grace which was given to us in Christ Jesus before time began,* [10]*but has now been revealed by the appearing of our Savior Jesus Christ, who has abolished death and brought life and immortality to light through the gospel,* [11]*to which I was appointed a preacher, an apostle, and a teacher of the Gentiles.* [12]*For this reason I also suffer these things; nevertheless I am not ashamed, for I know whom I have believed and am persuaded that He is able to keep what I have committed to Him until that Day.*

13Hold fast the pattern of sound words which you have heard from me, in faith and love which are in Christ Jesus. 14That good thing which was committed to you, keep by the Holy Spirit who dwells in us.

15This you know, that all those in Asia have turned away from me, among whom are Phygellus and Hermogenes. 16The Lord grant mercy to the household of Onesiphorus, for he often refreshed me, and was not ashamed of my chain; 17but when he arrived in Rome, he sought me out very zealously and found me. 18The Lord grant to him that he may find mercy from the Lord in that Day—and you know very well how many ways he ministered to me at Ephesus.

EXPLORATION

1. What can we learn from Paul's good attitude toward his difficult situation?

2. Why does God allow believers to suffer? How does Paul seem to answer this question?

3. What enables Christians to endure trials?

4. In what ways have you seen God protect and provide for his people?

5. What hope does this passage offer to people who are suffering?

INSPIRATION

A day in the life of Christ . . .

A day in which Jesus experiences more stress than he will any other day of his life—aside from his crucifixion. Before the morning becomes evening, he has reason to weep . . . run . . . shout . . . curse . . . praise . . . doubt. From calm to chaos. From peace to perplexity. Within moments his world is turned upside down . . .

The morning has been a jungle trail of the unexpected. First Jesus grieves over the death of a dear friend and relative. Then his life is threatened. Next he celebrates the triumphant return of his followers. Then he is nearly suffocated by a brouhaha of humanity. Bereavement . . . jeopardy . . . jubilation . . . bedlam . . .

Ponder this the next time your world goes from calm to chaos . . . Jesus knows how you feel.

A friend of mine was recently trying to teach his six-year-old son how to shoot a basket. The boy would take the basketball and push it as hard as he could toward the goal, but it always fell short. The father would then take the ball and toss it toward the basket, saying something like, "Just do it like this, son. It's easy."

Then the boy would try, and miss, again. My friend would then take the ball and make another basket, encouraging his son to push the ball a bit harder.

After several minutes and many misses, the boy responded to his father's encouragement by saying, "Yeah, but it's easy for you up there. You don't know how hard it is from down here."

You and I can never say that about God. Of the many messages Jesus taught us that day about stress, the first one is this: "God knows how you feel." (From *In the Eye of the Storm* by Max Lucado)

REACTION

6. Describe some of the problems and pain that Jesus experienced during his life on earth.

7. What difference does it make to us to know that Jesus dealt with many of the same emotions and troubles that we face?

8. If God knows how we feel, what keeps us from turning to him for comfort and help?

9. In what way does this passage change your attitude toward the problems you face today?

10. How can we help one another cope with life's difficulties?

11. What words of encouragement could you offer to a fellow believer who is suffering?

LIFE LESSONS

We can encourage (literally, "inject courage into") others in numerous ways as illustrated by Paul in his opening words to Timothy. We can trust them with our personal situation, allowing them to care for us. We can remind them of their heritage and history, the resources they have to face their circumstances. We can share how Christ motivates us, not because we are so successful but because of "his own purpose and grace." Someone you talk to today could benefit deeply from your encouragement.

DEVOTION

Lord, thank you for becoming flesh and blood, for being willing to face the stress and strain of daily life. It gives us strength and hope to know that you have gone before us and that you endured without giving up. Help us to remember that you understand our deepest longings, our heartaches, and our dreams.

For more Bible passages on suffering, see Job 36:15; Psalm 73:26; Romans 5:3–5; 8:17–18; Philippians 1:29–2:2; 3:10; 4:13; Hebrews 11:32–40; 1 Peter 4:12–16.

To complete the books of 1 & 2 Timothy and Titus during this twelve-part study, read 2 Timothy 1:1–18.

JOURNALING

When has God helped me through a painful experience in my life? How can I thank him?

PERSEVERANCE

MAX
LUCADO

REFLECTION

When you think of perseverance, who or what comes to mind? Think of someone you know who has shown courage and determination in a difficult situation. In what way has that person's example influenced you?

SITUATION

Part of the purpose of Paul's letter was to "hand off" to Timothy the ongoing responsibility for spreading the gospel. Timothy would no longer be on temporary assignments for Paul. He was now a journeyman minister. Paul included in his comments a formal charge to his friend and "son."

OBSERVATION

Read 2 Timothy 2:1–13 from the NCV or the NKJV.

NCV

¹*You then, Timothy, my child, be strong in the grace we have in Christ Jesus. ²You should teach people whom you can trust the things you and many others have heard me say. Then they will be able to teach others. ³Share in the troubles we have like a good soldier of Christ Jesus. ⁴A soldier wants to please the enlisting officer, so no one serving in the army wastes time with everyday matters. ⁵Also an athlete who takes part in a contest must obey all the rules in order to win. ⁶The farmer who works hard should be the first person to get some of the food that was grown. ⁷Think about what I am saying, because the Lord will give you the ability to understand everything.*

⁸*Remember Jesus Christ, who was raised from the dead, who is from the family of David. This is the Good News I preach,* ⁹*and I am suffering because of it to the point of being bound with chains like a criminal. But God's teaching is not in chains.* ¹⁰*So I patiently accept all these troubles so that those whom God has chosen can have the salvation that is in Christ Jesus. With that salvation comes glory that never ends.*

> ¹¹*This teaching is true:*
>
> *If we died with him, we will also live with him.*
>
> ¹²*If we accept suffering, we will also rule with him.*
>
> *If we refuse to accept him, he will refuse to accept us.*
>
> ¹³*If we are not faithful, he will still be faithful,*
>
> *because he cannot be false to himself.*

NKJV

¹*You therefore, my son, be strong in the grace that is in Christ Jesus.* ²*And the things that you have heard from me among many witnesses, commit these to faithful men who will be able to teach others also.* ³*You therefore must endure hardship as a good soldier of Jesus Christ.* ⁴*No one engaged in warfare entangles himself with the affairs of this life, that he may please him who enlisted him as a soldier.* ⁵*And also if anyone competes in athletics, he is not crowned unless he competes according to the rules.* ⁶*The hard-working farmer must be first to partake of the crops.* ⁷*Consider what I say, and may the Lord give you understanding in all things.*

⁸*Remember that Jesus Christ, of the seed of David, was raised from the dead according to my gospel,* ⁹*for which I suffer trouble as an evildoer, even to the point of chains; but the word of God is not chained.* ¹⁰*Therefore I endure all things for the sake of the elect, that they also may obtain the salvation which is in Christ Jesus with eternal glory.*

¹¹*This is a faithful saying:*

> *For if we died with Him,*
>
> *We shall also live with Him.*
>
> ¹²*If we endure,*
>
> *We shall also reign with Him.*
>
> *If we deny Him,*
>
> *He also will deny us.*
>
> ¹³*If we are faithless,*
>
> *He remains faithful;*
>
> *He cannot deny Himself.*

EXPLORATION

1. What responsibility do believers have to teach others what they have learned? How does this happen most effectively?

2. In what way does being a Christian compare to being a soldier, an athlete, or a farmer?

3. Why should we ~~patiently~~ endure the troubles we encounter in life?

4. In what way will God reward those who accept suffering?

5. What hope does Scripture offer to people who are struggling to remain faithful to God?

03/20 INSPIRATION

Since God is more moved by our hurt than our eloquence, he responds. That's what fathers do.

That's exactly what Jim Redmond did.

His son Derek, a twenty-six-year-old Briton, was favored to win the four-hundred-meter race in the 1992 Barcelona Olympics. Halfway into his semi-final heat, a fiery pain seared through his right leg. He crumpled to the track with a torn hamstring.

As the medical attendants were approaching, Redmond fought to his feet. "It was animal instinct," he would later say. He set out hopping, pushing away the coaches in a crazed attempt to finish the race.

When he reached the stretch, a big man pushed through the crowd. He was wearing a t-shirt that read "Have you hugged your child today?" and a hat that challenged, "Just Do It." The man was Jim Redmond, Derek's father.

"You don't have to do this," he told his weeping son.

"Yes, I do," Derek declared.

"Well, then," said Jim, "we're going to finish this together."

And they did. Jim wrapped Derek's arm around his shoulder and helped him hobble to the finish line. Fighting off security men, the son's head sometimes buried in the father's shoulder, they stayed in Derek's lane to the end.

The crowd clapped, then stood, then cheered, and then wept as the father and the son finished the race.

What made the father do it? What made the father leave the stands to meet his son on the track? Was it the strength of his child? No, it was the pain of his child. His son was hurt and fighting to complete the race. So the father came to help him finish.

God does the same. Our prayers may be awkward. Our attempts may be feeble. But since the power of prayer is in the one who hears it and not the one who says them, our prayers do make a difference. (From *He Still Moves Stones* by Max Lucado)

REACTION

6. Why are some people willing to endure anything for Jesus Christ?

7. What is the problem with trying to avoid trials? (See also 1 Peter 1:6–9 for a perspective on this question.)

8. In what way does your eternal hope help you persevere?

9. How can prayer make a difference in the way we view our problems?

10. Describe how your faith in God helped you persevere through a time of disappointment or discouragement.

11. In what way would you live differently if you did not believe in eternal life?

LIFE LESSONS

✶ Perseverance can be described as faith stretched out over time. But perseverance must be lived one day at a time. Jesus pointed out that each day has plenty of its own problems (Matt. 6:34). The athlete, soldier, and farmer that Paul uses to illustrate perseverance all must wait to see the results of their efforts. Immediate feedback and benefits are nice, but the most important aspects of life require waiting, and waiting requires faith and character. The lessons we learn in life don't reach their full purpose until we have passed them on to someone else.

DEVOTION

Father, when trials come, doubts tend to creep into our minds. We wonder whether we will feel your presence and experience your power. But you have promised to be with us always. So we ask you to help us depend on you to carry us through the tough times. Remind us that one day we will live with you, and give us the strength to persevere until that day.

For more Bible passages on perseverance, see Romans 5:3–4; 1 Corinthians 13:7; 1 Timothy 4:15–16; Hebrews 10:35–39; 12:1–3; James 1:2–4:12; 5:11; Revelation 2:2–3.

To complete the books of 1 & 2 Timothy and Titus during this twelve-part study, read 2 Timothy 2:1–13.

JOURNALING

In what area of my life am I tempted to give up hope?

LESSON NINE

WORKERS
PLEASING
TO GOD

MAX
LUCADO

REFLECTION

Think about your personal measurement of success. What questions do you use to decide if an effort in which you have been involved is worthwhile or successful? Consider how God measures success. Why and how do you think God chooses people for his work?

SITUATION

Paul was well aware of the dangers of false teachers and troublemakers in the church, and so he warned Timothy to watch for foolish talk and evil teaching. He urged Timothy to be a leader by the example of his life as well as by instruction. Paul continued to offer notes for how a servant of the Lord acts, as well as insights about the spiritual life.

OBSERVATION

Read 2 Timothy 2:14–26 from the NCV or the NKJV.

NCV

14Continue teaching these things, warning people in God's presence not to argue about words. It does not help anyone, and it ruins those who listen. 15Make every effort to give yourself to God as the kind of person he will accept. Be a worker who is not ashamed and who uses the true teaching in the right way. 16Stay away from foolish, useless talk, because that will lead people further away from God. 17Their evil teaching will spread like a sickness inside the body. Hymenaeus and Philetus are like that. 18They have left the true teaching, saying that the rising from the dead has already taken place, and so they are destroying the faith of some people. 19But God's strong foundation continues to stand. These words are written on the seal: "The Lord knows those who belong to him," and "Everyone who wants to belong to the Lord must stop doing wrong."

²⁰In a large house there are not only things made of gold and silver, but also things made of wood and clay. Some things are used for special purposes, and others are made for ordinary jobs. ²¹All who make themselves clean from evil will be used for special purposes. They will be made holy, useful to the Master, ready to do any good work.

²²But run away from the evil young people like to do. Try hard to live right and to have faith, love, and peace, together with those who trust in the Lord from pure hearts. ²³Stay away from foolish and stupid arguments, because you know they grow into quarrels. ²⁴And a servant of the Lord must not quarrel but must be kind to everyone, a good teacher, and patient. ²⁵The Lord's servant must gently teach those who disagree. Then maybe God will let them change their minds so they can accept the truth. ²⁶And they may wake up and escape from the trap of the devil, who catches them to do what he wants.

NKJV

¹⁴Remind them of these things, charging them before the Lord not to strive about words to no profit, to the ruin of the hearers. ¹⁵Be diligent to present yourself approved to God, a worker who does not need to be ashamed, rightly dividing the word of truth. ¹⁶But shun profane and idle babblings, for they will increase to more ungodliness. ¹⁷And their message will spread like cancer. Hymenaeus and Philetus are of this sort, ¹⁸who have strayed concerning the truth, saying that the resurrection is already past; and they overthrow the faith of some. ¹⁹Nevertheless the solid foundation of God stands, having this seal: "The Lord knows those who are His," and, "Let everyone who names the name of Christ depart from iniquity."

²⁰But in a great house there are not only vessels of gold and silver, but also of wood and clay, some for honor and some for dishonor. ²¹Therefore if anyone cleanses himself from the latter, he will be a vessel for honor, sanctified and useful for the Master, prepared for every good work. ²²Flee also youthful lusts; but pursue righteousness, faith, love, peace with those who call on the Lord out of a pure heart. ²³But avoid foolish and ignorant disputes, knowing that they generate strife. ²⁴And a servant of the Lord must not quarrel but be gentle to all, able to teach, patient, ²⁵in humility correcting those who are in opposition, if God perhaps will grant them repentance, so that they may know the truth, ²⁶and that they may come to their senses and escape the snare of the devil, having been taken captive by him to do his will.

EXPLORATION

1. List the characteristics of a worker who is pleasing to God.

One who says Yes.
Kind
Patient
Does not Quarrel
Good Teacher
Gentle
Un ashamed

2. Why should believers avoid foolish arguments?

Starts fights

04/03?

* 3. Why is consistent study of God's Word essential to the Christian life?

4. What kind of person does God use to fulfill his special purposes?

5. In what ways can believers help those who are confused about the truth?

INSPIRATION

In the shop of a blacksmith, there are three types of tools.

There are tools on the junkpile: outdated, broken, dull, rusty. They sit in the cobwebbed corner, useless to their master, oblivious to their calling.

There are tools on the anvil: melted down, molten hot, moldable, changeable. They lie on the anvil, being shaped by their master, accepting their calling.

There are tools of usefulness: sharpened, primed, defined, mobile. They lie ready in the blacksmith's toolchest, available to their master, fulfilling their calling.

Some people lie useless: lives broken, talents wasting, fires quenched, dreams dashed. They are tossed in with the scrap iron, in desperate need of repair, with no notion of purpose.

Others lie on the anvil: hearts open, hungry to change, wounds healing, vision clearing. They welcome the painful pounding of the blacksmith's hammer, longing to be rebuilt, begging to be called.

Others lie in their Master's hands: well-tuned, noncompromising, polished, productive. They respond to their Master's forearm, demanding nothing, surrendering all.

We are all somewhere in the blacksmith's shop. We are either on the scrap pile, on the anvil, in the Master's hands, or in the toolchest. (Some of us have been in all three.) From the shelves to the workbench, from the water to the fire . . . I'm sure that somewhere you'll see yourself . . . The rubbish pile of broken tools, the anvil of recasting, the hands of the Master—it's a simultaneously joyful and painful voyage.

And for you who make the journey—who leave the heap and enter the fire, dare to be pounded on God's anvil, and doggedly seek to discover your own purpose—take courage, for you await the privilege of being called "God's chosen instruments." (From *Shaped by God* by Max Lucado)

04/10

REACTION

6. How does God prepare us to serve him? What kinds of "tools" does he use to make us effective "tools?"

7. List some of the challenges and rewards of being a servant of God.

8. Use verse 20 to evaluate your usefulness to God. How has he gifted you for his purposes?

9. How can we determine whether our work pleases God? What, according to this passage, is God looking for in us?

10. What spiritual disciplines can keep us focused on doing what God wants us to do?

Prayer
Study
Worship

11. In what practical ways can you better equip yourself for God's service?

LIFE LESSONS

Paul says that one of our goals as Christians is to have a "pure heart." In this passage, he expands that basic concept by helping us see that we must *find* our place in the body of Christ and *fill* our place in the body of Christ. Even while we are learning what it means to serve, we can serve. We can take the expectations of others into account, but ultimately we want to fulfill God's purposes for us and receive his approval. A persistent desire to accomplish this flows from a pure heart.

DEVOTION

Thank you, Father, for working through people to accomplish great things for your kingdom. We appreciate the privilege of being called your people and being used by you. Purify our hearts and make us holy. Transform us into the kind of people suitable for your work, and use us for your special purposes.

For more Bible passages on becoming a worker pleasing to God, see John 6:27; 9:4; 1 Corinthians 3:5–9; 4:12; 2 Corinthians 5:9–10; Ephesians 4:12–13; Colossians 3:23; 1 Thessalonians 4:11–12; 5:12–13; 2 Thessalonians 3:6–13; 2 Timothy 4:5; Hebrews 6:10–12.

To complete the books of 1 & 2 Timothy and Titus during this twelve-part study, read 2 Timothy 2:14–26.

JOURNALING

In what area of my life do I need to purify myself for God's work?

FOLLOWING
THE TRUTH

MAX
LUCADO

_4/17_

REFLECTION

Think about and identify one or two of the values your parents tried to teach you when you were growing up. In what ways have those truths helped you throughout your life?

SITUATION

Writing from prison, Paul knew that he would soon be gone. He wanted to leave Timothy fully equipped for every challenge. He knew that when Timothy's vivid memories of their conversations and experiences faded, he would always need to rely on God's Word. Faced with the same realities, we, too, must be diligent in paying attention to God's Word.

OBSERVATION

Read 2 Timothy 3:1–17 from the NCV or the NKJV.

NCV

¹Remember this! In the last days there will be many troubles, ²because people will love themselves, love money, brag, and be proud. They will say evil things against others and will not obey their parents or be thankful or be the kind of people God wants. ³They will not love others, will refuse to forgive, will gossip, and will not control themselves. They will be cruel, will hate what is good, ⁴will turn against their friends, and will do foolish things without thinking. They will be conceited, will love pleasure instead of God, ⁵and will act as if they serve God but will not have his power. Stay away from those people. ⁶Some of them go into homes and get control of silly women who are full of sin and are led by many evil desires. ⁷These women are always learning new teachings, but they are never able to understand the truth fully. ⁸Just as Jannes and Jambres were against Moses, these people are against the truth. Their thinking has been ruined, and they have failed in trying to follow the faith. ⁹But they will not be successful in what they do, because as with Jannes and Jambres, everyone will see that they are foolish.

[10]But you have followed what I teach, the way I live, my goal, faith, patience, and love. You know I never give up. [11]You know how I have been hurt and have suffered, as in Antioch, Iconium, and Lystra. I have suffered, but the Lord saved me from all those troubles. [12]Everyone who wants to live as God desires, in Christ Jesus, will be hurt. [13]But people who are evil and cheat others will go from bad to worse. They will fool others, but they will also be fooling themselves.

[14]But you should continue following the teachings you learned. You know they are true, because you trust those who taught you. [15]Since you were a child you have known the Holy Scriptures which are able to make you wise. And that wisdom leads to salvation through faith in Christ Jesus. [16]All Scripture is given by God and is useful for teaching, for showing people what is wrong in their lives, for correcting faults, and for teaching how to live right. [17]Using the Scriptures, the person who serves God will be capable, having all that is needed to do every good work.

NKJV

[1]But know this, that in the last days perilous times will come:[2]For men will be lovers of themselves, lovers of money, boasters, proud, blasphemers, disobedient to parents, unthankful, unholy, [3]unloving, unforgiving, slanderers, without self-control, brutal, despisers of good, [4]traitors, headstrong, haughty, lovers of pleasure rather than lovers of God, [5]having a form of godliness but denying its power. And from such people turn away! [6]For of this sort are those who creep into households and make captives of gullible women loaded down with sins, led away by various lusts, [7]always learning and never able to come to the knowledge of the truth. [8]Now as Jannes and Jambres resisted Moses, so do these also resist the truth: men of corrupt minds, disapproved concerning the faith; [9]but they will progress no further, for their folly will be manifest to all, as theirs also was.

[10]But you have carefully followed my doctrine, manner of life, purpose, faith, longsuffering, love, perseverance, [11]persecutions, afflictions, which happened to me at Antioch, at Iconium, at Lystra—what persecutions I endured. And out of them all the Lord delivered me. [12]Yes, and all who desire to live godly in Christ Jesus will suffer persecution. [13]But evil men and impostors will grow worse and worse, deceiving and being deceived. [14]But you must continue in the things which you have learned and been assured of, knowing from whom you have learned them, [15]and that from childhood you have known the Holy Scriptures, which are able to make you wise for salvation through faith which is in Christ Jesus.

[16]All Scripture is given by inspiration of God, and is profitable for doctrine, for reproof, for correction, for instruction in righteousness, [17]that the man of God may be complete, thoroughly equipped for every good work.

4/24

EXPLORATION

1. What kinds of trouble will come in the last days? How do we see Paul's description at least ~~partly~~ present in our times?

2. What pulls us away from God?

3. In what ways should Christians be different from people who haven't come to believe in Christ for salvation?

4. In what ways can believers protect themselves from worldly pressures?

5. How does studying Scripture equip us for God's work? What's involved beyond having a copy of the Bible?

INSPIRATION

The apostle Paul warned that many will follow the false teachers, not knowing that in feeding upon what these people say they are taking the devil's poison into their own lives. Thousands of people in every walk of life are being deceived today. False teachers use high-sounding words that seem like the height of logic, scholarship, and sophistication. They are intellectually clever and crafty in their sophistry. They are adept at beguiling men and women whose spiritual foundations are weak.

These false teachers have departed from the faith of God revealed in the Scripture . . .

Writing to Timothy, the apostle Paul warned, "Now the Spirit expressly says that in latter times some will depart from the faith, giving heed to deceiving spirits and doctrines of demons, speaking lies in hypocrisy, having their own conscience seared with a hot iron."

Paul later wrote to Timothy, "For the time will come when they will not endure sound doctrine, but according to their own desires, because they have itching ears, they will heap up for themselves teachers; and they will turn their ears away from the truth, and be turned aside to fables." Doesn't this sound familiar today?

God's plan is not abstract or unclear. It is not a secret. He says very clearly, "I love you!" He has called tens of thousands all over the world to proclaim His love to the world and to call every man, woman, and child to His loving arms. To exemplify the army of God that is going forth at this moment into the world I can think of no better example than the thousands of "barefoot preachers" and other itinerant evangelists we helped train in Amsterdam during the past decade . . . Preachers, teachers, students, and mission helpers came from all over the world. Thousands came from Africa . . . They came from all over Asia, Latin America, and Eastern Europe, and they went out into the streets of Amsterdam to see and learn and share the love of Jesus Christ with others.

Today that mighty army of traveling preachers from every corner of the world is traveling from village to village and house to house preaching the Good News of God's love. Why do they do it? For the money? No, they receive almost no support for what they do. Many are lucky if they have a bicycle, a Bible, and a change of clothes. Do they do it for fame and fortune? There is none. In most cases only God knows what good works these humble, sincere pastors have done.

They do it because Jesus Christ is alive! He is living in their hearts, and that Good News is something worthy to share with the world. They are compelled by the life that is in them to tell everyone that Jesus is Lord. If Jesus Christ is *not* the Son of God, nothing matters. But if He is, *nothing else matters!* (From *Storm Warning* by Billy Graham)

REACTION

6. In what ways does our society distort God's truth?

7. How can bending or distorting God's truth hurt people?

8. What motivates you to trust and follow the teachings in God's Word?

9. For what reasons do some people reject or oppose the truth?

10. How can we guard the truth of the gospel?

11. List some specific ways you can show respect for God's Word this week.

LIFE LESSONS

Whether or not we are living in the actual last days, the practical side of this passage remains in full force: our lives must ultimately be guided by God's Word. Paul reminded Timothy (and us) that there are various "profitable" ways to apply Scripture. Every passage we read offers us one or more of the following gifts: truth (doctrine), conviction (reproof), direction (correction), and training (instruction in righteousness). But even knowing that God's Word has been given to accomplish these purposes in us is not enough. We must actually submit our lives to God's Word by knowing and obeying it.

DEVOTION

Father, we thank you for giving us your Word and for teaching us what is good and true. Keep us from deceptive teaching and twisted versions of the truth. May we guard our lives with the truth, for your Word is life.

For more Bible passages on guarding the truth, see Psalm 119:30; Proverbs 7:1–4; Acts 20:28–32; 1 Corinthians 16:13; 1 Timothy 6:20–21; 2 Timothy 1:13–14; 2:15–19, 23–25; 3 John 3–4.

To complete the books of 1 & 2 Timothy and Titus during this twelve-part study, read 2 Timothy 3:1–4:22.

JOURNALING

In what way do I need to follow God's truth more closely?

INTRODUCTION TO THE BOOK OF TITUS

The letter to Titus was the result of two storms.

The first was a storm that left Paul on the island of Crete (Acts 27). The second was a storm of relativism that left the Cretans with few values.

"Cretans are always liars, evil animals, and lazy people who do nothing but eat." The words didn't originate with Paul but might as well have. He used them to summarize the state of affairs on the island (Titus 1:12 NCV).

He had reason to lament. By the time of Paul, the society had a despicable reputation. Greed was god. Schemers were admired. Cheating was wrong only if you got caught. Right and wrong were determined by the situation, and rape was not a crime.

The economy was so bad that boys were sold as mercenaries as young as the age of twelve. Hence, the people were left with few male role models and fewer abiding beliefs.

Paul established the church in the society and sent Titus to "finish doing the things that still needed to be done." (1:5 NCV). Since Paul had definite ideas as to what still needed to be done, we are given definite principles of a healthy church.

Strong leadership is the first item. Titus is instructed to select elders and to do so carefully (1:4–16).

Strong character is the next. Judging from the style of life in Crete, it would have been easy for the Cretan Christians to compromise their convictions. Paul urges them not to.

Judging from the style of life in our world, we could do with the same reminder.

By the way, don't miss Paul's eloquent paragraph on grace (2:11–14). We're familiar with grace that saves, but grace does much more. It trains us "to live now in a wise and right way" (v. 12 NCV).

Something told Paul the Cretans needed such instruction. Something tells me that we do too.

5/22

LESSON ELEVEN

ROLE
MODELS

MAX
LUCADO

REFLECTION

Who do you consider to be your role models? In what ways have they influenced you for good?

SITUATION

When he wrote to Titus, many of the conditions in Paul's life were the same as when he wrote to Timothy. There was less history between Paul and Titus, but the elder trusted the younger with an important assignment on the island of Crete. Titus had the responsibility for shaping the church of Christ that was developing throughout the towns on the island.

OBSERVATION

Read Titus 2:1–15 from the NCV or the NKJV.

NCV

¹But you must tell everyone what to do to follow the true teaching. ²Teach older men to be self-controlled, serious, wise, strong in faith, in love, and in patience.

³In the same way, teach older women to be holy in their behavior, not speaking against others or enslaved to too much wine, but teaching what is good. ⁴Then they can teach the young women to love their husbands, to love their children, ⁵to be wise and pure, to be good workers at home, to be kind, and to yield to their husbands. Then no one will be able to criticize the teaching God gave us.

⁶*In the same way, encourage young men to be wise. ⁷In every way be an example of doing good deeds. When you teach, do it with honesty and seriousness. ⁸Speak the truth so that you cannot be criticized. Then those who are against you will be ashamed because there is nothing bad to say about us.*

⁹*Slaves should yield to their own masters at all times, trying to please them and not arguing with them. ¹⁰They should not steal from them but should show their masters they can be fully trusted so that in everything they do they will make the teaching of God our Savior attractive.*

¹¹*That is the way we should live, because God's grace that can save everyone has come. ¹²It teaches us not to live against God nor to do the evil things the world wants to do. Instead, that grace teaches us to live now in a wise and right way and in a way that shows we serve God. ¹³We should live like that while we wait for our great hope and the coming of the glory of our great God and Savior Jesus Christ. ¹⁴He gave himself for us so he might pay the price to free us from all evil and to make us pure people who belong only to him—people who are always wanting to do good deeds.*

¹⁵*Say these things and encourage the people and tell them what is wrong in their lives, with all authority. Do not let anyone treat you as if you were unimportant.*

NKJV

¹*But as for you, speak the things which are proper for sound doctrine: ²that the older men be sober, reverent, temperate, sound in faith, in love, in patience; ³the older women likewise, that they be reverent in behavior, not slanderers, not given to much wine, teachers of good things—⁴that they admonish the young women to love their husbands, to love their children, ⁵to be discreet, chaste, homemakers, good, obedient to their own husbands, that the word of God may not be blasphemed.*

⁶*Likewise exhort the young men to be sober-minded, ⁷in all things showing yourself to be a pattern of good works; in doctrine showing integrity, reverence, incorruptibility, ⁸sound speech that cannot be condemned, that one who is an opponent may be ashamed, having nothing evil to say of you.*

⁹*Exhort bondservants to be obedient to their own masters, to be well pleasing in all things, not answering back, ¹⁰not pilfering, but showing all good fidelity, that they may adorn the doctrine of God our Savior in all things.*

¹¹*For the grace of God that brings salvation has appeared to all men, ¹²teaching us that, denying ungodliness and worldly lusts, we should live soberly, righteously, and godly in the present age, ¹³looking for the blessed hope and glorious appearing of our great God and Savior Jesus Christ, ¹⁴who gave Himself for us, that He might redeem us from every lawless deed and purify for Himself His own special people, zealous for good works.*

¹⁵*Speak these things, exhort, and rebuke with all authority. Let no one despise you.*

EXPLORATION

1. What attitudes and behaviors should older men and women exemplify for the younger generations?

2. Why is it more effective to *show* people how to live than to *tell* them?

3. In what way can we attract others to the teaching of God?

4. How can you earn the right to give advice to others about how to live for God?

5. Why do Christian leaders deserve respect? In what ways can we express respect?

INSPIRATION

Now I see why powerful people often wear sunglasses—the spotlight blinds them to reality. They suffer from a delusion that power means something (it doesn't). They suffer from the misconception that titles make a difference (they don't). They are under the impression that earthly authority will make a heavenly difference (it won't).

Can I prove my point? Take this quiz.

Name the ten wealthiest men in the world.

Name the last ten Heisman trophy winners.

Name the last ten winners of the Miss America contest.

Name eight people who have won the Nobel or Pulitzer prize.

How about the last ten Academy Award winners for best picture or the last decade's worth of World Series winners?

How did you do? I didn't do well either. With the exception of you trivia hounds, none of us remember the headliners of yesterday too well. Surprising how quickly we forget, isn't it? And what I've mentioned above are no second-rate achievements. These are the best in their fields. But the applause dies. Awards tarnish. Achievements are forgotten. Accolades and certificates are buried with their owners.

Here's another quiz. See how you do on this one.

Think of three people you enjoy spending time with.

Name ten people who have taught you something worthwhile.

Name five friends who have helped you in a difficult time.

List a few teachers who have aided your journey through school.

Name half-a-dozen heroes whose stories have inspired you.

Easier? It was for me, too. The lesson? The people who make a difference are not the ones with the credentials, but the ones with the concern. (From *And the Angels Were Silent* by Max Lucado)

REACTION

6. List some ways we can show Christian concern for one another. (For ideas, see other passages like Romans 12:10; Colossians 3:12; and 1 Peter 3:8.)

7. What happens when believers reach out to help others in the family of God?

8. In what way can we find the strength and power to live righteously?

9. What motivates you to live for God?

10. Name someone who can help keep you accountable in your Christian walk. What do you think that accountability needs to involve?

11. Think of one person you can encourage in the faith. How would you do it?

LIFE LESSONS

People with a "big picture" view and a clear purpose can navigate the rough terrain of life. Those who walk through a wilderness will keep their path straight if they have a distant reference point. "Looking for the blessed hope and glorious appearing of our great God and Savior Jesus Christ" (2:13 NKJV). Christ is the only reference point that can be seen from any place in life and will surely guide us home. As Paul reminds us, we're not walking through the wilderness alone. We journey with lots of company. Believers younger and older than ourselves. People in different seasons of life, different spheres of influence. How we choose to get along as we make our way indicates how carefully we are keeping our eyes on Jesus, our hope (see Hebrews 12:1–2).

DEVOTION

Thank you, Father, for the role models you have given us. Remind us that our actions and attitudes can make a real difference in the lives of others, either for good or for bad. We pray, Father, that you would empower us by your Holy Spirit to set a positive example for others to follow.

For more Bible passages on setting a good example, see 2 Thessalonians 3:9; 1 Timothy 4:12; Hebrews 12:3; James 5:10; 1 Peter 2:21.

To complete the books of 1 & 2 Timothy and Titus during this twelve-part study, read Titus 1:1–2:15.

JOURNALING

What do my daily actions and attitudes reveal about my beliefs?

LIFE IN THE SPIRIT

MAX LUCADO

REFLECTION

Think of one person who lives what you consider a Spirit-filled life. Consider how that person approaches obstacles and difficulties along the way. Note how he or she relates to other people. What evidences of God's power do you see in that person's life?

SITUATION

In contrast to his fatherly style with Timothy, Paul was able to communicate in a brief, almost memolike style to Titus. There was little concern for the younger man's feelings or struggles. Perhaps he was older than Timothy and had proven his abilities. Paul issued his directives to Titus in a tone of expectation. Titus carried out Paul's instructions with the blessing of the apostle and the encouraging greetings of those with him.

OBSERVATION

Read Titus 3:1–15 from the NCV or the NKJV.

NCV

¹Remind the believers to yield to the authority of rulers and government leaders, to obey them, to be ready to do good, ²to speak no evil about anyone, to live in peace, and to be gentle and polite to all people.

³In the past we also were foolish. We did not obey, we were wrong, and we were slaves to many things our bodies wanted and enjoyed. We spent our lives doing evil and being jealous. People hated us, and we hated each other. ⁴But when the kindness and love of God our Savior was shown, ⁵he saved us because of his mercy. It was not because of good deeds we did to be right with him. He saved us through the washing that made us new people through the Holy Spirit. ⁶God poured out richly upon us that Holy Spirit through Jesus Christ our Savior. ⁷Being made right with God by his grace, we could have the hope of receiving the life that never ends.

⁸This teaching is true, and I want you to be sure the people understand these things. Then those who believe in God will be careful to use their lives for doing good. These things are good and will help everyone.

⁹But stay away from those who have foolish arguments and talk about useless family histories and argue and quarrel about the law. Those things are worth nothing and will not help anyone. ¹⁰After a first and second warning, avoid someone who causes arguments. ¹¹You can know that such people are evil and sinful; their own sins prove them wrong.

¹²When I send Artemas or Tychicus to you, make every effort to come to me at Nicopolis, because I have decided to stay there this winter. ¹³Do all you can to help Zenas the lawyer and Apollos on their journey so that they have everything they need. ¹⁴Our people must learn to use their lives for doing good deeds to provide what is necessary so that their lives will not be useless.

¹⁵All who are with me greet you. Greet those who love us in the faith.

Grace be with you all.

NKJV

¹Remind them to be subject to rulers and authorities, to obey, to be ready for every good work, ²to speak evil of no one, to be peaceable, gentle, showing all humility to all men. ³For we ourselves were also once foolish, disobedient, deceived, serving various lusts and pleasures, living in malice and envy, hateful and hating one another. ⁴But when the kindness and the love of God our Savior toward man appeared, ⁵not by works of righteousness which we have done, but according to His mercy He saved us, through the washing of regeneration and renewing of the Holy Spirit, ⁶whom He poured out on us abundantly through Jesus Christ our Savior, ⁷that having been justified by His grace we should become heirs according to the hope of eternal life.

⁸This is a faithful saying, and these things I want you to affirm constantly, that those who have believed in God should be careful to maintain good works. These things are good and profitable to men.

⁹But avoid foolish disputes, genealogies, contentions, and strivings about the law; for they are unprofitable and useless. ¹⁰Reject a divisive man after the first and second admonition, ¹¹knowing that such a person is warped and sinning, being self-condemned.

¹²When I send Artemas to you, or Tychicus, be diligent to come to me at Nicopolis, for I have decided to spend the winter there. ¹³Send Zenas the lawyer and Apollos on their journey with haste, that they may lack nothing. ¹⁴And let our people also learn to maintain good works, to meet urgent needs, that they may not be unfruitful.

¹⁵All who are with me greet you. Greet those who love us in the faith.

Grace be with you all. Amen.

EXPLORATION

1. Based on these verses, what are some of the ways our lives should change after we become believers?

2. How does sin enslave people?

3. Why are good deeds unable to make a person right with God?

4. What does Christ's saving work do for people who accept him?

5. Explain how the Holy Spirit can make someone a new person.

INSPIRATION

Can a scientist study stars and never weep at their splendor? Dissect a rose and never notice its perfume? Can a theologian study the Law until he decodes the shoe size of Moses but still lack the peace needed for a good night's sleep? Maybe that's why Nicodemus comes at night. He is tired and can't sleep. Tired of rules and regulations but no rest. Nicodemus is looking for a change. And he has a hunch Jesus can give it.

Though Nicodemus asks no question, Jesus offers him an answer. "Truly, truly, I say to you, unless one is born again he cannot see the kingdom of God" (John 3:3 NASB).

This is radical language. To see the kingdom of God you need an unprecedented rebirth from God. Nicodemus staggers at the elephantine thought. "How can a man be born when he is old? He cannot enter a second time into his mother's womb and be born, can he?" (v. 4 NASB) . . .

Nicodemus seems to be saying, "Jesus, I've got the spiritual energy of an old mule. How do you expect me to be born again when I can't even remember if figs can be eaten on the Sabbath? I'm an old man. How can a man be born when he is old?" According to Christ, the new birth must come from a new place. "The truth is, no one can enter the Kingdom of God without being born of water and the Spirit. Humans can reproduce only human life, but the Holy Spirit gives new life from heaven" (vv. 5–6 NLT).

Could Jesus be more direct? "*No one* can enter the Kingdom of God without being born of water and the Spirit." You want to go to heaven? Doesn't matter how religious you are or how many rules you keep. You need a new birth; you need to be "born of water and the Spirit."

God gives no sponge baths. He washes us from head to toe. Paul reflected on his conversion and wrote: "He gave us a good bath, and we came out of it new people, washed inside and out by the Holy Spirit" (Titus 3:5 MSG) . . .

When you believe in Christ, Christ works a miracle in you. "When you believed in Christ, he identified you as his own by giving you the Holy Spirit" (Eph. 1:13 NLT). You are permanently purified and empowered by God himself. The message of Jesus to the religious person is simple: It's not what you do. It's what I do. I have moved in. And in time you can say with Paul, "I myself no longer live, but Christ lives in me" (Gal. 2:20 NLT). (From *Next Door Savior* by Max Lucado)

REACTION

6. Explain the role of the Holy Spirit in renewing and equipping believers. (See also Luke 10:21; John 14:26; Acts 4:31; and 2 Peter 1:21.)

7. What does it mean to be led by the Spirit? How is the presence of the Holy Spirit like an internal GPS guidance system?

8. What role does the Holy Spirit play in your life?

9. Why is it important to remember that we are saved by God's grace, not by anything that we have done?

10. If we are saved by faith, not works, why should we work to live righteous lives?

11. What happens when we try to do what is right in our own strength instead of depending on the Holy Spirit to help us? Describe a personal experience that illustrates the point for you.

LIFE LESSONS

Unless you've memorized 1 & 2 Timothy and Titus during this study, you've discovered there are simply too many practical guidelines in these brief letters to remember them all. Depending on your place in life, you may want to review the letters often and list the guidelines that particularly apply to your relationships and duties. In his closing to Titus, Paul highlights the particular role of each person in the Trinity in our salvation—God our Father, Jesus Christ our Savior, and the Holy Spirit our Renewer. Everything we do and have flows out of what God has already done.

DEVOTION

Forgive us, Father, for thinking that we can make things right with you on our own. It is through your grace alone that we stand before you. We need your help even to live for you. Fill us with wisdom, renew our hearts and minds, and attune our ears to your Spirit's voice. Let our lives be testimonies of your Spirit's power.

For more Bible passages on living in the Spirit, see John 14:15–17; Acts 1:8; 2:17–18, 38–39; Romans 8:4–17, 26–27; 1 Corinthians 3:16; 12:13; Galatians 5:25; 2 Peter 1:21.

To complete the books of 1 & 2 Timothy and Titus during this twelve-part study, read Titus 3:1–15.

JOURNALING

How can I thank God for the changes his Spirit has made in my life?

Lucado Life Lesson Series

| The Gospel of Mark | The Gospel of Luke | The Gospel of John | Acts |
| 1-4185-0942-6 | 1-4185-0943-4 | 1-4185-0944-2 | 1-4185-0945-0 |

| Romans | 1 Corinthians | Ephesians | Hebrews |
| 1-4185-0946-9 | 1-4185-0947-7 | 1-4185-0953-1 | 1-4185-0955-8 |

| James | 1 & 2 Timothy and Titus | 1 & 2 Peter | Revelation |
| 1-4185-0956-6 | 1-4185-0954-X | 1-4185-0957-4 | 1-4185-0958-2 |

Revised and updated, the Lucado Life Lessons series is perfect
for small group or individual use and includes intriguing questions
that will take you deeper into God's Word.

NELSON IMPACT
A Division of Thomas Nelson Publishers
Since 1798

Available at your local Christian Bookstore